Don't Ask And I Won't Have To Lie

50 is the New 30 and Other Tall Tales

BEVERLY MAHONE

Benoham Publishing
A Division of BAM Enterprises

Don't Ask And I Won't Have To Lie
50 is the New 30 and Other Tall Tales

Copyright © 2010 by Beverly Mahone

Copyedit by: Sandra Holcombe
SDH Productions
sdhproductions@juno.com

Book layout by: Ginger Marks,
DocUmeant Designs
www.DocUmeantDesigns.com

Benoham Publishing
P.O. Box 11037
Durham, NC 27703
www.talk2bev.com

ISBN-13 978-0-9778876-2-0 $12.95
ISBN-10 0-977-8876-2-6

Printed in the United States of America

First Printing

Dedication

This book is dedicated to:

My three-year-old grandson as a heads-up on the lies he's bound to hear from females at various times in his life.

Every woman over 40 who has ever lied.

Don't Ask and I Won't Have to Lie is written for informational and entertainment purposes only and not meant to psychoanalyze the deeply rooted issues that may have manifested the turmoil in your life and led to your lying habits.

I do not have the answers to your problems. You need a shrink for that!

Table of Contents

If God was not a forgiving God, most of us, if not all, would be denied entrance into Heaven because of one sin:

Thou Shall Not Lie

Dear Lord,

I told a few more lies today
That I did not mean to tell
When the bill collector called
I told him the check was in the mail.

When my girlfriend asked how
Her new hairdo looked
I was forced into another untruth
"You paid for that?!" I wanted to say
But that would've been uncouth.

And then there was the lie I told myself
When I went shopping for the perfect dress
"I'll fit into this size 10—no problem
It's just a matter of exercise and eating less."

Lord, I am asking for your forgiveness
For the truth I always seem to bend
Although it's never my intention to lie
I'm sure I probably will again.

AMEN

Don't Ask and I Won't Have to Lie

If you do not wish to be lied to, do not ask questions. If there were no questions, there would be no lies.

~Author B. Traven

Acknowledgements

I want to express my sincere gratitude to the following women who contributed to this book by sharing their own "lies." As you can see, some of the names were changed to protect the innocent:

Jazzy147, Jeanie52, Judy Davids (aka Rock Star Mommy), Kayzmarie, KK, Pam, and Simplycr.

I also want to thank Debra Stokes, Sharon Williams, Linda J. Alexander, Natasha Petersen, and Paulette Thorpe who helped move the book writing process along by giving me their two cents and more when I asked for it.

Dr. Trevy McDonald is a book full of knowledge and insight. She is always my go-to person when I need an honest assessment of my writing.

The folks at BettyConfidential.com deserve big kudos for the comprehensive survey they did on the lies women tell and granting me permission to use their results as a part of my research.

A research paper co-written by Dr. Gail Heyman, a Professor in the Department of Psychology at the University of California, San Diego, was the inspiration behind chapter two in this book. Thanks, Dr. Heyman, for allowing me to draw from your knowledge, along with Diem Luu, a former UCSD student, and Professor Kang Lee from the University of Toronto.

I can't say enough about the outstanding work of Ginger Marks of DocUmeant Designs. From the moment you talk with Ginger about your project, she gives a one thousand percent effort. I recommend her highly for all your graphic design and publishing needs.

Finally, no book I ever write could be complete without expressing my love and appreciation for my husband, Nathaniel. He continues to be the wind beneath my wings and has truly made an honest woman out of me.

Don't Ask and I Won't Have to Lie

Introduction

When I was in my twenties, I recall receiving some advice that I've never forgotten. I was told there were three things a woman should never admit:

1) How old she really is
2) How much she makes
3) How much she makes out

I don't think I ever gave much thought as to why I shouldn't reveal this information back then, but it is a liar's motto that I still relate to as a woman now in her fifties.

The idea for *Don't Ask And I Won't Have To Lie* was conceived in 2008, the moment I walked out of my doctor's office. To make a long story short, I told her a lie and got caught. That lie nearly cost me my life because I was in denial about the reality of my midlife medical issues. I was also afraid to face the possible consequences of my actions.

It's funny how time changes people and circumstances. Back in my younger, single, and healthier days, my fears amounted to such things like whether or not I would get caught cheating on a boyfriend, if a potential husband discovered how many sexual partners I really had, or how many times I could proclaim to be a virgin. I discovered I could always lie my way around those situations with little or no consequences or concern.

These days, however, I am convinced that lying, not honesty is the best policy for entirely different reasons. I'm not talking about malicious, hateful lies. I'm referring to the "stories" we tell to protect friends, loved ones, and even ourselves from hurt, pain, depression, anger, conflict, and embarrassment.

Sometimes we, as middle-aged women, find ourselves in situations where we just don't want to deal with the reality of a particular situation, so we conceal it with our own distorted viewpoint. That is, in essence, what I did with some health issues I was dealing with. I preferred not to face the seriousness of my midlife medical crisis, so I convinced myself I could manage my own health-care regimen instead of following a physician's strict guidelines. I also feared how my illness would be perceived by my employer as it related to my job performance and to my soon-to-be husband—so I just kept lying to myself until those lies caught up with me.

The idea of growing older in a society where youth and beauty are depicted as a thing to behold can also resort in a cover-up. That might explain why women over 40 account for nearly half of all cosmetic surgery routines in the United States. Some go to great lengths to conceal what they believe are physical flaws because, as an over zealous media always reminds us, image is everything.

Then you have some women who fear what telling the truth would do to their long-standing marriages, friendships, and other relationships. Can you imagine what 62 year old actress Meredith Baxter went through all those years before she finally revealed publicly that she was a lesbian? The married-three-times, mother of five was quoted as saying she held on to the secret for several years before finally coming forward with the truth. (Actress Meredith Baxter says she's a lesbian, 2009)

Don't Ask And I Won't Have To Lie explores some of the subjects we lie about, why we do it, and the role aging plays in the process.

This book is not meant to defend anyone's need to fib, but it may help you understand the reasons behind some of the untruths you hear.

What's better: a lie that draws a
smile or
the truth that draws a tear?

1. The Truth Hurts or Does It?

Some twenty-five years ago, I made a terrible mistake by telling the TRUTH to a girlfriend about her womanizing boyfriend.

To make a long story short, my girlfriend wanted to know what I thought of the new man in her life. Instead of lying and saying something like, "He seems like a good match for you," I had to go and tell her the truth. I believed she deserved to know about his flirtatious behavior and how he tried to get me to sneak away for a rendezvous during her 30th birthday party.

But rather than see him for the scumbag that he was, she turned around and accused me of being the seductress. She questioned what I had said or done to entice him. I became the villain and her archenemy. Needless to say, we stopped speaking.

That incident made me wonder if there were, indeed, circumstances where it was okay to lie. I never had any intention of hurting my friend—and I certainly didn't want to see her get hurt by a man who seemed to show little respect for her love.

Not long ago, I heard from her. She called out of the blue to chat for old time's sake. You know I was dying to find out whatever happened to what's-his-name, but the subject never came up during the conversation. I was really curious to know how long she put up with his crap after our falling out.

But you know what? Even if they were still together today, I would just let sleeping dogs lie and say in my most enthusiastic voice, "You go, girl!" After all, if she managed to put up with him after all of this time, who was I to burst her bubble, right?

Growing older has definitely made me more mindful of something I call "liar's etiquette." That means knowing how delicately the lie you tell must be handled under certain circumstances. If I were faced with the same situation today, I'm sure I wouldn't blab to her like I did back then, but you can believe I would definitely confront her so-called boyfriend and give him a piece of my mind.

Would not telling her make me a bad girlfriend? No, because sometimes it's better to protect a friend or loved one by withholding the truth. There's nothing malicious or deceitful about that.

What do you think?

We lie to protect ourselves; we lie to promote ourselves. We lie to elevate ourselves; we lie to excuse ourselves.

~ Dr. Chuck Borsellino

2. Because Mommy Said So

To understand why we lie, we need not look any further than our own mothers. They are the ones who taught us how to lie and when those lies were appropriate. Of course we, as little girls, never wanted to believe our mommies would do such a thing, but they did—just as their mothers more than likely lied to them.

The experts call it parenting by lying. (Heyman, Luu, & Lee, Volume 38, Issue 3 September 2009) It's a strategy—and a very successful one I might add—used to manipulate a young child's behavior and emotions. Our mothers warned us about all the bad things that would happen if we didn't do what they told us to do. They even conned us into good behavior all year long by reminding us that Santa Claus wouldn't bring us any toys if we were naughty.

Once, my inquiring mind wanted to know how Santa was able to get into our home since we had no chimney. How was I to know at the time that my mother was telling a bold-faced lie when she said Santa had a special key to unlock the door?

The trauma of losing my baby teeth was always glossed over with a visit from the Tooth Fairy, who never failed to leave a nice, shiny quarter. How was I to know there was no such creature who had wings, could fly up to my second-floor bedroom, unlock the window, come in, sneak a quarter under my pillow and be gone without making a sound?

On the flip side: What about those times our mothers forced us to lie to them? They told you not to do something. You did it anyway. They confronted you. What did you do? You lied so you wouldn't get in trouble.

Isn't it ironic that our moms spent so much time preaching "honesty is the best policy" while steadily lying to us about this or that? The other irony is the fact that sometimes their lies were meant to protect us from hurt or just to make us happy. In a strange kind of way this could be perceived as a part of a mother's nurturing process.

There was the time I remember making an ashtray as my Mother's Day gift. It looked okay going into the kiln, but when it came out of the fiery furnace, it looked more like a foreign object. Despite my embarrassment, disappointment, and tears, I painted it red, wrapped it up, and gave it to Lillian.

When she opened her gift, you would've thought I had given her a piece of gold jewelry with the way she reacted. She kept talking about how beautiful it was and placed it right on the coffee table in the living room for everyone to see.

To this day, she still has that little red ashtray I made in kindergarten 47 years ago—plus another ugly pink one I made in first grade. That's one lie I was very happy to hear.

What lies do you remember your mother telling you as a child? Do any of these sound familiar:

- "This is going to hurt me more than it hurts you."

- "If you sit too close to the TV, you'll go blind."

- Eat your carrots so you'll have perfect vision."

- "The stork brought you."

- "If you swallow a watermelon seed, it will grow inside your stomach."

- "Drinking coffee will stunt your growth."

- "If you don't eat all of your food, you will get pimples."

- "We took Fluffy (your dead pet) to live on a farm in the country so he could have other animals to play with."

- If you don't go to bed on time, the bogeyman will get you.

■■■

After becoming a mother more than 20 years ago, I started to understand the methodology of lying to your child. Just like my mom, I used Santa Claus for behavior modification and instead of a nice, shiny quarter, my fictitious tooth fairy left one-dollar bills under my daughter's pillow at night. I figured with inflation and all, her teeth deserved a raise.

And yes, just as my mother lied to protect my feelings from being hurt over those ashtrays and probably some other things I've forgotten about, I also stretched the truth to protect my own child from harm. For example, even when I knew my marriage to her father was over, I continued to keep up appearances in front of her (and the general public) so she would think of us as one very happy family and be the envy of all her friends from single-parent homes.

I confess that was definitely one hard lie to maintain until I finally stopped the nonsense with a divorce.

As I became an older parent, I spent less time lying for behavior modification and more time on covering up my daughter's flaws—as well as my own as her mother.

I might also add that the parenting-by-lying theory also works for grandparents.

I have a three-year-old grandson that I lie to right now. He's too young to believe his dear, sweet grandma would ever tell him anything but the truth, the whole truth and nothing but the truth—but he's at the age where he needs behavior modification. Since I'm his primary caregiver while his mom's away at college, it's my responsibility to keep him in check with a few lies when necessary.

For example, if I get a call from his daycare telling me he's been misbehaving, I tell him he won't be allowed to go to soccer practice if he keeps acting up. That always seems to straighten him up, even though I know I'm lying when I say it.

When he starts feeling sad about not having his mommy around and says, "I want my mommy to come home from college," I tell him, "Jesus wants your mommy to go to college so she can get smarter, get a job, and take care of you." It sounds nice, doesn't it?

The truth of the matter is I want his mother—my daughter—to get a degree and get a job so she can take her son and get out my house. I want her to prove that I did a pretty decent job in raising her to make it on her own. Lord knows, I don't want to spend the next 10 to 20 years of my life covering up her shortcomings as an adult.

Unfortunately, some mothers do just that. They lie to keep others from knowing the truth about what's really going on with their grown children. Not long ago, I experienced this with someone from my childhood. She found me on Facebook and followed up with a telephone chat. When I asked about her family, she proceeded to tell me that her son had graduated from college with honors and was doing very well as a CPA. Surprisingly, I later learned this woman's son had dropped out of college, was unemployed, and still living at home with his mother. Why she felt the need to lie about her son was beyond me, but I guess she figured I'd never find out since we don't socialize in the same circles or live in the same state for that matter.

I, too, have been guilty of lying on behalf of my daughter. I was forced to do it when she was a high school freshman. I started getting letters and phone calls about her cutting classes, so I decided to nip it in the bud by sending her to another school where she wouldn't be so easily influenced. Unfortunately, my school of choice was on the other side of town and out of our designated district. To accomplish this mission, I had to write a letter to our local school board to request a transfer from one high school to another.

Initially, I told the truth by letting the board know I was interested in my daughter getting a quality education—and it wasn't happening at her current school. That request was denied, but I had the right to appeal, which I did. In a face-to-face meeting, I had to resort to lying by telling a three-member panel my daughter wanted to go into the engineering program and the school she was currently attending didn't offer it. Request APPROVED. Between you and me, she never took one class in that engineering department.

I might also add that I would've never had to lie if quality schools existed no matter what side of the tracks you live on. Have you ever noticed how the better schools go hand-in-hand with the pricier neighborhoods? Why should any child be denied a quality education just because their parents can't afford to live in a certain area? Of course, that's a story for another book.........

On a lighter note, I will say having a child was a big plus for lying when I worked in Corporate America as a single mom. I can't count the number of times I used the story of having a "sick child" as an excuse because I didn't want to go into work on a particular day. No one would dare question whether that was a lie or not, especially since they all knew about my no-good, dead-beat WAS*band*. I was definitely a repeat offender, but I learned how to moderate that lying habit so it would always work to my advantage.

Surely, I'm not the only one who's ever done that, right?

With lies you may get ahead in the world—but you can never go back.

~Russian Proverb

3. And The Survey Says...

You and I will tell an average of 88,000 lies over the course of our lives, according to a 2008 London survey. This amounts to 1,460 untruths a year, or more than four lies a day if you live to be 60 years old. If these numbers are correct, that means I've already told close to 76,000 lies.

At least once a day I pretend I'm not home when the telephone rings. Is it just me? How many times have you looked at the number on the caller ID before making a decision as to whether you were going to answer it or not? Many of my girlfriends say if they don't recognize the number they are more inclined not to answer it for fear that it could be a bill collector or nagging telemarketer. Even when they do recognize the number, they can still ignore it and no one would be the wiser.

Speaking of pretending—I had an experience at church not long ago that made me question the honesty and sincerity of some people who call themselves Christians. To make a long story short, one night, during a revival meeting, two female church members I know walked past me and my grandson in the parking lot without speaking but made it a point to greet everyone else in our immediate vicinity. In my mind, I wondered what I had ever done to receive their cold shoulder. Once inside, these same two women were throwing their hands up, praising God and shouting hallelujah during the service. Then I wondered who were they lying to—themselves or God? You see, my pastor has this saying: "How can you love a God you never see and then refuse to speak to your neighbor whom you can see?" I'm just saying...

So what are some of the other things you and I are guilty of lying about? Weight, age, image, quality of life, and sexual experience top the list according to a number of surveys and research studies. In a comprehensive *Feel the Pulse of Women*™ survey conducted by BettyConfidential.com, weight was the number one thing women said they lied about. (April Daniels Hussar & Julie Ryan Evans, 2008) That's a lie every woman can get away with because who's going to know if you skim ten or fifteen pounds from your actual weight? Is someone going to demand that you get on a scale to prove or disprove it? Besides, we all know those things are always inaccurate.

Another way to lie about those frustrating pounds is to simply camouflage it. That's so much easier to do than to keep making the same old New Year's Resolution to lose weight. I used to do that. Every January 1, I was always motivated and energized to lose the weight. Sometimes I even started my exercise routine the week after Christmas to give my body a head start. But by the middle of February, when the scales weren't moving anymore, I didn't seem to be moving much either. But now I save myself the heartache by going out and buying extra large one-size-fits-all tent tops, dresses and stretch pants. If you can't see the fat it doesn't exist, right?

One of my girlfriends says she hasn't gained one pound on her driver's license in over 10 years. I'd say that's pretty remarkable since she went up two dress sizes during that same time frame.

When it comes to lying about age, some women say if they can get away with proclaiming to be ten years younger or more, that suits them just fine because the thought of adding another year to their age can be depressing. That certainly explains why some women go to great lengths to look as young as they claim to feel.

I'm actually one of those women who stopped lying about my age as I got older. I played that game as a teenager while trying to impress the older boys. Fifteen turned into seventeen and eighteen became twenty-one on quite a few occasions.

I'll also tell you that I played a similar game with toilet paper and went from a 32AA to a 36B under my cheerleader sweater.

In 2010 I'm happy to accept my fifty-something years as a badge of honor, and—although it took me a long time and some extra weight to do it—I've finally grown into that 36B.

The one study that surprises me comes from researchers at the University of Massachusetts. They claim women are more often to lie about their sexual experiences by minimizing the number of partners they've had. I understand this might be a delicate subject for younger women since no one wants to be thought of as a Sleep-Around-Sue when you're trying to find your Mr. Right; however, at our age it's a different story.

I mean, what inquiring minds really want to know about the number of intimate relationships we're having in our forties, fifties, and sixties? Our parents? Our children? Why should we tell them? I'm not saying it's okay to sleep with every Tom, Dick, or Harry that comes your way. Discretion is always important, but if you're single, divorced, or widowed, whose business is it if you've had five or fifteen lovers? The only person who needs to hear that truth is your gynecologist.

Oh what a tangled web we weave,
When first we practice to deceive.

~Sir Walter Scott

4. Lying Can Be Hazardous To Your Health

After being diagnosed with congestive heart failure, hyperthyroidism, and hypertension a little more than 10 years ago, I was placed on a very strict health care regimen that was forcing me to make drastic changes in my everyday lifestyle. My heart, I was told, was very weak, and the other medical problems exacerbated my overall condition.

I had a hard time dealing with that diagnosis because I certainly didn't see myself on a death bed at the age of 40. I also had difficulty coming to grips with the reality that I had to take the very same medication that really old, sick people needed to stay alive. All of these thoughts, coupled with the fact that I hate taking pills, became an excuse for skipping dosages. I figured if I missed a pill or two once or twice a week it was no big deal. After all, I was taking the medication the majority of the time, so it was in my system.

Little did I know that not following the doctor's orders was causing my body serious harm.

One day during a visit to my cardiologist, I lied about taking all of the medication as prescribed. Subsequently, my blood tests revealed the truth by disclosing the fact that not taking the pills as recommended had weakened my heart, raised my blood pressure, and caused my TSH (thyroid stimulating hormone) levels to reach an all-time record high. According to my doctor, if I had continued the same pattern of pill-taking and lying, it could have cost me my life.

Whew! That was certainly not a lie worth dying over. Besides, as a woman entering her midlife journey, I had plenty to live for. I just married a hot, new man; my first grandchild was on the way; and I was entering a new world of entrepreneurship.

At that moment, I learned a very important lesson.

YOU SHOULD NOT LIE TO YOUR DOCTOR.

According to a 2007 Columbia University survey, 52 percent of women ages twenty-five to forty-nine said they had no problem telling small fibs to their doctors. Nearly two-thirds of those surveyed said the reasons they lie are because they didn't want their doctors to give them a lecture, and 38 percent just didn't want to feel judged.

The survey further revealed sometimes the lies women told their doctors weren't intentional. Some patients misunderstood the questions. For instance, when asked what medications they took, they never thought to include vitamins, which are forms of medication.

What I discovered was lying or omitting the facts to your doctor can be hazardous to your health. You just need to come clean.

Here are some of the most common lies we are guilty of telling, according to a survey in Redbook Magazine: (Dworkin-McDaniel, 2008)

"I don't drink" or "I don't drink often."

If you're on any type of medication, you owe it to your doctor to come clean about your alcohol intake. You could have a bad reaction by mixing drugs and alcohol. Doctors say drinking in excess (more than ten to fourteen drinks per week) may increase the risk of breast cancer and cardiovascular disease. Menstrual disorders have also been associated with heavy drinking, and continued drinking can lead to early menopause.

"I exercise regularly."

Okay, we know that muscle weighs more than fat, but if you've gained 20 pounds in a year, you may be exercising your mouth more than your body. If you are, indeed, exercising consistently, it's important to let your doctor know exactly what type of exercises you're doing and how much you're eating as well. You may need a nutritionist to help you.

"I don't smoke" or "I smoke less than a pack a day."

I have a friend who smokes like a chimney and there's no amount of perfume, chewing gum, or breath mints to cover the cigarette smell. If I can smell it as a novice, why would you think your doctor couldn't?

"I'm not sexually active."

Like I said in the previous chapter, the only person who really needs to know your sexual history and habits is your gynecologist. But it IS important information to divulge. Lying about the number of partners you've had can be detrimental, especially if you develop an STD or AIDS. The best advice is to keep it real with your doctor.

"I don't do drugs."

Lying about drug use is just as, if not more, dangerous than lying about your alcohol intake. Mixing certain medications with over-the-counter drugs can dilute the effectiveness of the medication you need to cure whatever illness or disease you may be suffering from.

That's why it's important to tell the doctor about all the pills you take—whether they are prescribed or not.

In a study published in the December 2008 *Journal of the American Medical Association,* one in twenty-five adults between the ages of fifty-seven and eighty-five put themselves at risk for major drug interactions by mixing prescription drugs with over-the-counter medications such as aspirin, vitamins, and supplements.

I believe if you're serious about your health, honesty is always the best policy, but I also understand the fear that can be associated with telling the truth, the whole truth, and nothing but the truth. In my case, I preferred not to face the seriousness of my midlife medical crisis, so I convinced myself I could manage my own health care just as well, instead of following a physician's strict guidelines. I also feared how my illness would be perceived by my employer as it related to my performance, so I just kept lying to myself until those lies caught up with me.

I admit I'm still skipping my medication on occasion, due to forgetfulness, but I'm not lying about it to my doctor anymore.

Lying about my age is easier now
since I sometimes forget what it is!

~Anonymous

5. Fifty is the New What?

Barbara Walters from Daytime TV's *The View* sure looks fabulous for an 80-year-old woman, doesn't she? She doesn't look a day over 50. I wonder what her secret is. Okay, I know what her secret is and you do too. She is among a group of older women who have discovered a new fountain of youth. Surely you've heard about the new campaign to convince us that *50 is the new 30* and *40 is the new 20*—so that must mean *80 is the new 50*.

As a former television reporter, I know first-hand how important looks are in the news business. While it seems perfectly acceptable to have a gray-haired, not getting any younger, male anchor deliver the news, the belief is no one wants to see a mature-looking, slightly wrinkle-faced woman in the same position.

And she can't weigh more than 130 pounds because anyone who's ever been on television will tell you the studio cameras add at least ten pounds to your body. If you don't believe me, just look at the current female anchors in your local community. How many of them are over 50 and fat?

The fear of aging has caused many middle-aged women to resort to all sorts of lying tactics in an effort to turn back the hands of time. The goal is to look as young as you can for as long as possible. That's because there is a lot of anguish attached to growing older. It means we are not viewed as attractive or thought of as eye candy anymore. It also means we are closer to death.

We look in the mirror and see gray hair, wrinkles, and sagging skin. We see the reflections of our mother's faces—tired and worn from years of neglect and stress. That reality staring back at us calls for drastic measures.

To make matters worse, we are constantly bombarded with messages and images of what is considered sexy and appealing on television, magazines, and, yes, even in our fairy tales. You remember the story of Snow White? When the mature, stately looking queen gazed into the mirror and asked who was the fairest in the land, the mirror replied:

You, my queen, are fair; it is true. But (younger) Snow White is fairer than you.

That response sent the queen into a rage as she plotted to kill Snow White with a poison apple.

Of course, women aren't going to that extreme in real life; however, to keep up with a youth-obsessed society, some feel compelled to do whatever it takes to turn back the aging clock. Facelifts, breast augmentation, and tummy tucks are just a few of the cosmetic procedures designed to help reclaim the Fountain of Youth.

Ever had a girlfriend go away on vacation and when she came back, she looked refreshed and several years younger? When you asked her about it, she told you it was R&R (rest and relaxation) that did it. She wouldn't dare confess to the cosmetic surgery that helped give her a stunning new look.

A number of older women even admit to undergoing plastic surgery so they could feel competitive in today's job market. According to a Dr. Mauro Romita, a plastic surgeon in New York, women in their 40s and 50s want to look younger, have a better appearance, and not to look tired. They believe a touch-up here and there, along with their work experience, can give them a distinct advantage

Meanwhile, according to the American Society of Aesthetic Plastic Surgery (ASAPS), there were close to 10 million cosmetic procedures in 2009, with women accounting for 91 percent of ALL procedures. Here are some other facts from the ASAPS: (American Society of Aesthetic Plastic Surgeons)

- Americans spent nearly $10.5 billion in 2009 on various cosmetic procedures.

- A total of 4.4 million women between the ages of thirty-five and fifty had liposuction—representing 45 percent of all procedures.

- Eyelid surgery was performed on 2.6 million women between the ages of fifty-one and sixty-four.

Even though my mother never went under the knife to get rid of her fat, she took part in the big cover up. She was forever trying to squeeze her size 16 body into a 36-inch girdle. How about you? Do you own a pair of Spanks or the Ardyss Body Magic?

And what else might you be covering up?

- When you take off your makeup, will people still recognize you?

- Are your eyes really brown but you're wearing "colored" contacts?

- Is your hair longer and because of hair extensions?

- Did you decide to perk up your sagging breasts with breast implants?

- What is the REAL color of your hair— or does only your hair dresser know for sure?

- For African-American Women only: Who told you blond was your color?

Two women I applaud for being forthright and honest about all the plastic surgery they've had are comedienne Joan Rivers, and the self proclaimed "Queen of all Media," Wendy Williams.

Rivers, now in her 70s, says ever since she was a child she was always insecure about her looks. As a result, she's reportedly had at least two facelifts, an eye tuck, Botox and liposuction. She's also been the butt of her own cosmetic surgery jokes by poking light humor at the fact that her husband committed suicide the same night she was undergoing her liposuction procedure. Rivers says her motto is: "better a new face coming out of an old car than an old face coming out of a new car."

Wendy Williams has also had her share of procedures that reportedly included a boob job, tummy tuck and liposuction. She was quoted in New York Magazine saying her D-cup implants gave her breasts the size that her self-image required. She added, "I know I'm not perfect, but plastic surgery has allowed me the freedom mentally to be me."

For those women, unlike Joan and Wendy, who can't afford to spend money on a nip and tuck, there's, what I call, instant cosmetic surgery in a jar, tube, or bottle. Women spend an average of $12,000 a year on things like make up, hair care, and anti-aging creams. All, of which, are designed to either enhance overall beauty or create an illusion.

Speaking of anti-aging creams, I'm not convinced they actually work. Are you? Personally, I don't think you can eliminate wrinkles with those products. I think you just get smoother wrinkles.

While I don't advocate lying about your age or the extremes one will go to in an effort to maintain a youthful look, I do understand some of the reasons behind it. Growing older can be a scary thought. In addition to the physical changes we face, it can also take an emotional toll. No one should have to spend their remaining years fretting over fading beauty.

I am of the opinion, however, that, as we age, we should become more accepting of our appearance. I have learned to accept the fact that a big butt runs in my family gene pool and my small bust size just means more than a handful is wasted.

This is the time we, as middle-aged women, should be digging deep to discover our inner beauty and let it shine with wisdom, strength, and experience.

Please don't kid yourself—fifty isn't anything new. Instead of trying to convince yourself that it is with a lift, a tuck or some miracle anti-aging cream, why not follow some great advice offered by the late actress Rosalind Russell:

Taking joy in living is a woman's best cosmetic.

I have no problem with lies of omission, as I don't believe everyone needs to know everything."

~Mitch Mitchell

6. Maybe It's None Of Your Business

How many times have you said "I'm fine" when someone asked how you were doing, knowing it wasn't the truth? Your intention was not to lie, but you just might not have been in the mood to talk about what's going on in your world.

I've been there and done that many times. Does the fact that I refuse to tell you my real feelings mean I'm lying? According to the *Feel the Pulse of Women*™ survey conducted by BettyConfidential.com, fifty-five percent say they do not consider withholding information a lie. (April Daniels Hussar & Julie Ryan Evans, 2008)

On the other hand, one might argue that hiding the truth is actually a lie of omission—leaving out something you shouldn't have.

At midlife there are a number of reasons why we'd rather say "Everything is okay" than to go into the details of what may be a disappointing, sad or stressful life. Many of us go out of our way to hide our mistakes and failures. Sometimes who we are is not what we want everybody to see. We don't want anyone to find out that our lives aren't as picture perfect as we try to paint them. We dare not let anyone see our unhappiness.

If you have the image of being in a happy marriage, why should anyone find out that there is no romance and intimacy between you anymore or that he has committed adultery? As long as he's taking care of home, nothing else is necessary to discuss.

When media reports surfaced about the break-up between Tipper and Al Gore after forty years of marriage, I immediately wanted to know what happened. To the general public, they were a very happy couple; however, a published email reportedly sent by the Gores made it obvious that no one knew what was going on behind closed doors:

"...after a great deal of thought and discussion, we have decided to separate. This is very much a mutual and mutually supportive decision that we have made together following a process of long and careful consideration (Allen, 2010)

One has to wonder just how long they had been keeping up appearances—for appearance sake.

But here's the thing: they are not the only married couple in the same or a similar situation. There are wives everywhere hanging on to their marriage vows. Some may choose to remain in bad situations because it's easier to stay and tolerate than to pack up and try to start all over again. Others may not believe in the idea of getting a divorce so they stick it out *until death do us part* literally. Finances may also be a motive—like it was in my previous marriage.

I had grown accustomed to the lifestyle we were living and didn't want to give it up, despite the fact that the thrill was gone. Even though I was making a decent salary on my own, I didn't see how I could survive financially as a single parent. Another thing, I didn't want to be viewed as a failure in the marriage department since all my girlfriends seemed to be living in wedded bliss. I kept trying to convince myself I could hang in there for money's sake until I finally realized money can't buy love and happiness or keep a cold bed warm at night.

It's funny how I can admit that now, but back then it was nobody's business.

Something else I can admit now is what I went through to keep my teenage daughter's pregnancy a secret. When I first suspected she was pregnant, I went into a state of denial. I didn't want to believe nor accept the fact that my baby was having a baby.

I did everything in my power to shield her from the public so no one would find out. Our mother-daughter weekends, complete with shopping sprees, stopped abruptly. We became no-shows at church and I even canceled the big wedding I had spent nearly a year planning. The rumor mill was allegedly churning at my church with the "I've been saved all my life and never messed up" Christians whispering behind my back about my parenting skills and wayward daughter.

I was concerned about what my friends and acquaintances would think of me. You see, I was the old-school mom who was quick to criticize other people's children for being fast and loose and not having good moral values. I was also the one constantly preaching, "Keep your dress down and your panties up!" The fact that my daughter didn't heed my advice was a poor reflection of my child-rearing skills in my mind. I was too angry, hurt and embarrassed so I chose to remain isolated and not be confronted with the truth.

Once I finally accepted the reality of my daughter's pregnancy, and was able to talk about it, I could move forward. I'll be perfectly honest though—it wasn't easy, but having a wonderful, "I'm in this with you," husband and a couple of really close, non-judgmental friends helped out a lot. Plus, I now have a beautiful grandson who is simply amazing.

What truths have you been unwilling to deal with or accept?

Perhaps you're a woman over 40, still single and still looking for Mr. Right. Are you willing to share how alone you feel and how often you cry at night due to the lack of companionship? Maybe you're jealous of your married girlfriends and wish you had what they have.

I actually got mad at one of my girlfriends because she re-married before I did. To add insult to injury, she didn't even ask me to be a member of her wedding party. Do you think I ever told her how I felt?

Have you been battling serious bouts of anxiety and depression that may have led to a drug or alcohol addiction? Maybe you're in denial about the seriousness of the problem.

Could you be totally honest about your secret drinking habits? You may call yourself a social drinker but the real truth is if someone knew how much you drink weekly or even daily, they would suggest Alcoholics Anonymous. Addiction Psychiatrist, Dr. Robert Swift, says, "It's more common among women to hide their drinking because of the social stigma attached to it."

Are you, what I call, emotionally constipated? You have a lot of blockage in your mind and heart that keeps you from moving forward.

You, in turn, blame others for your shortcomings and failures instead of owning up to your self-made mess.

Here's what I think: With aging comes a no-holds-barred attitude—where you feel like you can finally get "stuff" off your chest. You should no longer worry about expressing your true feelings, especially if it will help someone else grow, become a better person or help you with a personal breakthrough.

On the other hand, if your need to lie serves as a form of protection from feelings of hurt, pain, guilt, grief, frustration, etc., then you say what you want to.

So the next time someone asks, "How are you today,"...how will you respond? As for me, I think I'll give it to them straight with no chaser!

"Honesty is the first chapter of the book of wisdom." ~Thomas Jefferson

"Today I bent the truth to be kind, and I have no regrets, for I am far surer of what is kind than I am of what is true."

~Robert Brault

7. Miscellaneous Lies

- "Girl, your hair looks so good." – Lie! You are thinking, "What is she going through to wear her hair like that?"

- "Nooo, Girl, that outfit is not too snug." – Lie! You're thinking that if she has even a half glass of water, all the seams will bust.

- "Call me anytime if I can help." – Lie! Please don't call. I just said that to be polite.

- "No, I don't mind at all." – Lie! I really do mind keeping her six terrible acting kids.

Submitted by JB

I started a rock band in my 40s with no musical experience. After about five practices, I was in a bar telling this guy with bravado, "I'm in a band." I loved the way that statement rolled off my tongue. Then he said, "Oh really? I book bands. Can you play next Wednesday?" I said, "Yes."

The truth was, we only knew two songs. I told my bandmates I booked us a show and they wanted to kill me. We weren't ready. But you know what? That lie forced us to raise the bar, and we learned enough songs and we played. It was the best lie I ever told. Only our audience was punished for that lie. We sucked that night, but it gave us confidence that we really were a band, and it also made me an honest woman.

Submitted by Judy Davids

■ ■

I've been lying to my husband since we began dating and cannot understand why. Before we got married he asked me how many sexual partners I had before him. I told him 3, when in fact, it was more like 10.

When asked what age I lost my virginity, I replied 17, when in reality it was 16. I don't believe the disparity in a year made any difference.

I still say my weight is the same as listed on my driver's license, 137 pounds, when it's actually more like 145.

I consider these social lies to safeguard my husband's perception of me. It's not a betrayal but a little white lie. Would he really care to know the truth at this point in our 13-year marriage?

Name Withheld

■■■■■■■■■■■■■■■■■■■■■■■■■■■■■■■■■■■■■■■

It's my birthday and I've just received a handmade gift from a dear friend. It's got to be the ugliest pair of slipper socks imaginable. I tell her, "I love them," and thank her. How could I hurt my friend's labor of love and friendship?

Submitted by Kayzmarie

∎∎∎∎∎∎∎∎∎∎∎∎∎∎∎∎∎∎∎∎∎∎∎∎∎∎∎∎∎∎∎∎∎∎∎∎∎

A very good friend told me about a new haircut and color she just had, and couldn't wait for me to see it. She was beyond excited. When I finally saw her, my jaw dropped to the floor. It was awful! The cut was too short and made her face look fat and the color was way too brassy and washed out her complexion. She felt sassy and adorable.

Would I shatter her illusion by telling her the truth? Not on your life! If she felt delicious about herself, I was not going to spoil it. I told her she looked ten years younger and the smile on her face told me I had said the right thing.

Submitted by "KK"

∎∎∎∎∎∎∎∎∎∎∎∎∎∎∎∎∎∎∎∎∎∎∎∎∎∎∎∎∎∎∎∎∎∎∎ı

I had to lie many times to my son's ex-girlfriend after they broke up. She was a stalker. It was over but she just kept calling, and I would intercept the calls for him. Finally she gave up. I guess she found someone else.

Submitted by Jeanie52

∎∎∎∎∎∎∎∎∎∎∎∎∎∎∎∎∎∎∎∎∎∎∎∎∎∎∎∎∎∎∎∎∎∎∎ı

When people asked me why I was getting a divorce, I lied because there was no point in airing dirty laundry in public. What he wanted and did was wrong, but I didn't feel it was something the rest of the world, particularly my grown children, needed to know. So I would say, "We grew apart," and that was partially true; I just didn't add the rest.

Submitted by Pam

■■■■■■■■■■■■■■■■■■■■■■■■■■■■■■■■■■■■

After my 87-year-old uncle was sent to a nursing home, I vowed to visit him at least three times a week. I became ill as a result of a heart condition but didn't want to worry him, so I told him I had a cold and didn't want to give it to him. I think a "white lie" to spare someone's feelings or protect one from harm is acceptable.

Submitted by Jazzy147

■■■■■■■■■■■■■■■■■■■■■■■■■■■■■■■■■■■■

I pray daily that there is a place in Heaven for every secretary who has ever had to tell a lie for her boss.

Submitted by Simplycr

■■■■■■■■■■■■■■■■■■■■■■■■■■■■■■■■■■■■■■ ı

Appendix A: Liar's Journal

Here's a fun exercise you can do. Over the next two weeks, write down all the lies you've told or heard from family members, friends, co-workers, in the media, etc. on the blank pages provided here. If you didn't tell or hear any on a specific day, leave it blank. If you heard or told more than one a day, be sure to record it.

For added fun, invite your girlfriends to participate.

After the two-week period is over, plan a get together to discuss _Don't Ask and I Won't Have To Lie_. You can make a game out of it by swapping books randomly and trying to guess which lies are connected to which girlfriend.

Note: Sunday is a FREE day. No, that doesn't mean you're free to tell all the lies you want or need to. Smile.

Week 1

<u>Monday</u>

Tuesday

_____

_____

_____

_____

_____

_____

_____

_____

Wednesday

_____

_____

_____

_____

_____

_____

_____

_____

_____

_____

Thursday

_____

_____

_____

_____

_____

_____

_____

_____

_____

Friday

_____

_____

_____

_____

_____

_____

_____

_____

_____

Saturday

_____

_____

_____

_____

_____

_____

_____

_____

_____

Week 2

Monday

_____

_____

_____

_____

_____

_____

_____

_____

_____

Tuesday

_____

_____

_____

_____

_____

_____

_____

_____

_____

Wednesday

_____

_____

_____

_____

_____

_____

_____

_____

_____

Thursday

_____

_____

_____

_____

_____

_____

_____

_____

_____

Friday

_____

_____

_____

_____

_____

_____

_____

_____

_____

Saturday

_____

_____

_____

_____

_____

_____

_____

_____

_____

Appendix B: The Comforting Girlfriend's Survey

What kind of girlfriend are you? How far would you go to protect your girlfriend's feelings?

Prior to completing this book, I decided to conduct a little survey to see how women would respond in situations involving their girlfriends. More than 100 women offered their responses.

Here are the questions. How would you respond?

1) If you were meeting your 60-year-old girlfriend for lunch at a trendy restaurant and she came in wearing some skin tight jeans, low cut shirt, flashy jewelry and

enough make-up for both of you, what would you say?

a) Nothing   27%

b) You would poke a little fun at her outfit, but only in the sweetest way   59%

c) You would suggest leaving the restaurant and going to a movie instead   2%

d) You would compliment her ability to dress like a 20-year-old.   12%

2) Your girlfriend's husband makes some inappropriate sexual comments to you while drinking at a party you're all attending. Do you:

a) Run and tell your girlfriend immediately

5.1%

b) Say nothing   36.4%

c) Threaten to tell your girlfriend if he does it again   0%

d) Tell him to call you later   59.6%

3) Your 55-year-old girlfriend wants your blessing for her relationship with a 25-year-old she's been dating for a couple of weeks. The word around town is he's a gigolo. What do you do?

a) Tell your girlfriend what you've heard 61%

b) Give her your blessing   9%

c) Set him up by making a pass at him and them telling your girlfriend how he responded   1%

d) Suggest you go out on a double date so you can get to know him better   9.2%

4) You've just learned your girlfriend is cheating on her husband and now she wants you to cover for her. What do you do?

a) Do it for her   4.1%

b) Have a heart-to-heart talk and try to talk her out of the affair   85.7%

c) Tell her husband anonymously   1%

d) Do it for her once but tell her you'll never do it again.   9.2%

5) Your girlfriend comes to the Company Christmas party wearing a hideous outfit with Christmas decorations attached. Everyone is talking behind her back about how ridiculous she looks. What do you do?

a) Ignore them   13.3%

b) Defend your friend by reminding everyone they're here to have fun and shouldn't worry about what someone else is wearing   64.3%

c) Pull your girlfriend to the side and tell her what others are saying   13.3%

d) Run out to a nearby store and find some decorations to attach to your own outfit 9.2%

---

6) You and your girlfriend's husband have been meeting secretly to plan a surprise birthday party for her. Another friend arouses suspicion by telling her she's seen the two of you together on several occasions. Unbeknownst to you, he lied about where he was going every time the two of you met. What do you do when your girlfriend confronts you?

a) Confess about the birthday party plan

41.4%

b) Deny it was you   0%

c) Tell her he was helping you plan a surprise party for your husband who just got a promotion at work (so you don't spoil her big surprise)   44.4%

d) Tell her the friend is mistaken—it wasn't you and she should trust her husband   14.1%

7) While you're at the grocery store, you see your friend's husband having a cozy

---

conversation with an unidentified woman in the Produce section. Later on, while talking with your girlfriend she tells you her husband saw you but you didn't speak. What do you do?

a) Tell her you didn't see him   32%

b) Tell her you wanted to but he was involved in a conversation with another woman   57.7%

c) Say nothing to her but later call her husband and threaten to tell his wife about the other woman   1.0%

d) Tell her you didn't recognize him   9.3%

8) You and your 40-year-old girlfriend go shopping and she tries on a dress that seems two sizes too small. What do you tell her when she asks how she looks in it?

a) "You look fabulous!"   0%

b) Tell her jokingly, "Try skipping a few meals before you wear it out." 7%

c) Buy a matching dress also two sizes too small so you'll look like twins 1%

d) Suggest she try a larger size 92%

9) Your 60-year-old girlfriend decides to change her hair color from a nice silver gray to platinum blonde and it looks a mess. What do you tell her?

a) "It's your hair honey. Do what you want."17%

b) Recommend she go to the salon for a makeover 8%

c) Suggest she purchase a wig instead 0%

d) Be honest. In the long run, she'll thank you for it. 75%

10) Your 65-year-old girlfriend has just told you she thinks she's a lesbian and is attracted to you. What do you do?

a) Thank her for the compliment   20%

b) Congratulate her   0%

c) Tell her you'll help her find someone   6%

d) Tell her thanks but no thanks   74%

11) If a friend shared some shameful, damage-your-reputation kind of information about a mutual girlfriend, would you feel compelled to tell her?

Yes   43.3%

No   56.7%

OK here's what I think:

1) If your 60-year-old girlfriend still looks sexy at her age without cosmetic surgery and the outfit proves it, why not compliment her. Suggesting you leave the restaurant and go to a movie, where it's dark inside, may suggest you're ashamed to be seen with her in public.

2) If you run and tell your girlfriend, she may turn the tables and accuse you of being the aggressor—especially if you've been drinking too. It's best to just say nothing and protect her feelings.

3) Give her your blessing first and then suggest you go out on a double date. Think how much fun that would be!

4) Do it for her. After all, what are girlfriends for? They keep your secrets and protect your feelings. If she doesn't think she's doing anything wrong, why should you?

5) If you ignore them, you will be silently agreeing with them and how will that make your girlfriend feel if you did not come to her defense?

7) It's a tossup between a) and d). Just because he says he saw you doesn't mean you saw him and he's not going to try to

prove you wrong if he was with someone he doesn't want his wife to know about.

8) You don't have to wear the dress—she does, so flatter your friend by complimenting her taste in clothes, while gently suggesting she try a larger size.

9) Give your girlfriend an ego boost by letting her know how much more fabulous she will look with a professional hairstylist doing her hair—and offer to pay for it as an early birthday gift or a "just because."

10) First and foremost, thank her for the compliment and then congratulate her on discovering her inner self.

Appendix C: Thank You

A special thank you to the following women who took the Comforting Girlfriend's Survey. For those of you who took it but do not see your name here, please forgive me:

Angie Baker, Eileen Bauer, Marcia Barhydt, Jeryl Brown, Dr. Glenda Clare, Angela Beyer Coulter, Sharon Darden, Teri Dempski, Jennifer Evans, Holly Gilger, Constance Harris, Donna-maria Harris, Dr. Gail Hayes, Heather K. Hyde-Herndon, Michelle Norman-Jasper, Deborah D. Jenkins, Evelyn Kalinosky, Kerry Kimble, Angel Lebak, Nancy Mattison, Michelle Mauldin, Sharon McMillan, Heidi Richards Mooney, Carine Nadel, Monique Oliver, Natasha Petersen,

Roxanne Ravenel, Elizabeth Roberts, Rosalind Sedacca, Gazelle Simmons, Wanda Smith, Brenda Spruell, Deb Stevens, Debra Stokes, Izora Summons, Rita Sweet, Gigi Washington, Barbara Jo Williams.

Appendix D: Resources

The following is a list of resources I used for some of the references in my book.

Siren Magazine
Why Vanity Keeps Us Poor by Molly Faulkner-Bond April 2007

Lifestyle Lift Cosmetic Surgery Center

Survey Monkey
Comforting Girlfriends Survey

Works Cited

Actress Meredith Baxter says she's a lesbian. (2009, December). Retrieved 2010, from Reuters: http://www.Reuters.com

Allen, M. (2010, June 1). *Al and Tipper Gore to Separate*. Retrieved 2010, from Politico.com: www.politico.com/news/stories/0610/38001.html

American Society of Aesthetic Plastic Surgeons. (2008). *Statistics*. Retrieved 2010, from Cosmetic Plastic Surgery Statistics: http://www.cosmeticplasticsurgerystatistics.com/statistics.html

April Daniels Hussar, D. E., & Julie Ryan Evans, E.-A.-L. (2008, August). *Feel the Pulse of WomenTM Survey*. Retrieved 2010, from Betty Confidential: http://www.BettyConfidential.com

Dworkin-McDaniel, N. (2008, October). *The Lies Women Tell Their Doctors*. Retrieved 2010, from Redbook Magazine: http://www.Redbookmag.com

Heyman, D. G., Luu, D. H., & Lee, P. K. (Volume 38, Issue 3 September 2009). *Parenting By Lying*. The Journal of Moral Education.

More about Beverly Mahone

Beverly is the host of a weekly talk/music show called The Boomer Beat on WCOM Radio in Carrboro, North Carolina (1035.5FM).

Through her social media marketing skills, Beverly created Boomer Diva Nation; an online community made up of women over 40 who represent the baby boomer woman. She is also a member of the Vibrant Nation Blog Circle, Boomer Authority, Boomer-Living and can also be found on Facebook, Twitter and LinkedIn.

She is also the inspiration behind Boomer Diva TV—an internet video site which she calls the place you can get "educated and entertained in less than five minutes."

Beverly has been classified as a baby boomer expert by the media and appeared on numerous radio and talk programs including:

WOR Radio in with Henican and White (New York City)

The Audrey Chapman Show (Washington, DC)

Madison in the Morning Sunny 93.9 (Raleigh, NC)

Just 4 Us with Gayle Hurd Foxy 107/104 (Raleigh, NC)

The Louie Jones Show (Chicago)

Chat with Women (Washington State)

MSNBC-TV   Boomer Nation

WGHP Fox 8 (High Point, NC)

WCCB Fox 18 (Charlotte, NC)

WTTG Fox 5   (Washington, DC)

SCE-TV   (Columbia, SC)

New York Times Newspaper Article June 7, 2007

She is also a popular blogger:

www.boomerworld.blogspot.com
www.babyboomerbev.blogspot.com
www.talk2bev.blogspot.com
www.makeyourmesyourmessage.wordpress.com
www.menopausemama.wordpress.com

You may also visit her websites:

www.beverlymahone.com
www.boomerdivanation.org